AF127541

UK GARAGE EXPLODED ONTO THE UK MUSIC SCENE IN THE MID'90S, EMERGING FROM THE VIBRANT WORLD OF LONDON'S NIGHTCLUBS AND PIRATE RADIO STATIONS.

THE GENRE DREW HEAVILY FROM AMERICAN GARAGE HOUSE, BLENDING ITS SOULFUL GROOVES WITH THE UK'S OWN R&B AND JUNGLE INFLUENCES, WHICH DOMINATED THE SOUNDSCAPE AT THE TIME.

UK GARAGE QUICKLY BECAME A CULTURAL PHENOMENON, SPARKING NEW GENRES LIKE GRIME, DUBSTEP AND BASSLINE, LEAVING AN INDELIBLE MARK ON BRITISH MUSIC HISTORY.

IN THIS VOLUME WE CONTINUE EXPLORING THE UK GARAGE SCENE BY SPOTLIGHTING 40 MORE RECORD LABELS - FROM UNDERGROUND PIONEERS TO CHART-TOPPERS, AND EVEN A FEW LEGENDARY NAMES THAT HAVE SINCE GONE SILENT.

THIS BOOK IS HERE TO DOCUMENT, ARCHIVE AND CELEBRATE THE LABELS THAT HELPED DEFINE, SHAPE AND EXPAND THE LEGACY OF UK GARAGE AND THOSE PUSHING THE SCENE INTO THE FUTURE.

Words
Chris Dexta

Editor
Colin Steven

Design
Banana Gun

Publishers
Southside Circulars
& Velocity Press

First edition
November 2024

southsidecirculars.com
velocitypress.uk

VP046

ISBN: 978-1-913231-70-5

THE ICON CATALOGUE
UK GARAGE
VOL. 2

01. 500 REKORDS
02. ALLSTARS
03. AZULI
04. BABYSHACK
05. BACK 2 FRONT
06. BIG APPLE
07. BUG RECORDS
08. CATCH
09. CHOCOLATE BOY
10. CITY DUB TRAXX
11. CONFETTI RECORDS
12. DEA PROJECT
13. DFL (DJ'S FOR LIFE)
14. E1 RECORDINGS
15. EC2A
16. FIFTY FIRST RECORDINGS
17. FLATTRAX
18. GD4YA
19. GHOST
20. GROOVE CHRONICLES
21. HARRY LIME
22. HOTPOINT
23. I! RECORDS
24. KRONIK RECORDS
25. LARGE JOINTS
26. LIFESTYLE
27. LONG LOST BROTHER
28. MONIE MUZIK
29. NEW DEAL RECORDINGS
30. NICE 'N' RIPE
31. NORTH WEST 10
32. POINT BLANK
33. QUENCH
34. RELENTLESS
35. S2S RECORDINGS
36. SHUFFLE'N'SWING
37. SMOKIN BEATS
38. TIMEHERI
39. UNIT FIVE RECORDS
40. URBAN BEAT

500 REKORDS

1996 - 2003

A cutting-edge UK Garage label that never missed, run by Earl Buchanan and Paul Chambers (aka New Horizons), predominantly releasing their own music. In fact, it was the only place to get their music!

THE ESSENTIALS
NEW HORIZONS 'FIND A PATH'
IN~SINC 'COOL THE MENTA'

ALLSTARS

1999 - 2000

Straight-up 2-Step UK Garage bootleg
remixes of contemporary popular music
from the same period, produced and run by
Steve Gurley (Rogue Unit) and Chris Mack
(Potential Bad Boy).

THE ESSENTIALS
ALLSTARS 'HOTBOY'
ALLSTARS 'WALK ON BY'

AZULI

1997 - 1999

A House and Garage label run from above
Black Market Records in Soho, which began
releasing UKG in 1997, featuring tracks and
remixes from Bump & Flex, Grant Nelson, Todd
Edwards and Tuff Jam, to name a few.

THE ESSENTIALS
INDO 'R U SLEEPING (BUMP & FLEX REMIX)'
PEPPER MACHE 'HAPPINESS (HAPPY DUB MIX)'

BABYSHACK

1996 - 1999

Not the most prolific of labels, but every release was on point, exploring all angles of the scene. They reached the charts with 'Bump 'n' Grind' - while also producing some seriously rare underground cuts!

THE ESSENTIALS
M DUBS 'BUMP'N'GRIND'
VINCENT J.ALVIS 'BODY KILLIN (M-DUBS BREAK BEAT FUNK RAP)'

BACK2FRONT

1997 - 1999

back2front

Releasing only five records in its two-year existence, Back 2 Front is a highly sought-after label, home to the 2-step classic 'Hyperfunk,' as well as some lesser-known but equally tasty beats from Antonio.

THE ESSENTIALS
ANTONIO 'HYPERFUNK (BONUS BEATS)'
URBAN GROOVERS 'TELL ME HOW'

BIG APPLE

2001 - 2002

Right at the tail end of the UKG golden era,
Big Apple literally took the darker, bass-heavy
vibes from the scene and laid the foundations
for Grime and Dubstep, with Artwork, Benga and
Digital Mystikz at the forefront.

THE ESSENTIALS
ARTWORK 'RANK'
BENGA 'DOSE'

BUG RECORDS

1997 - 2005

"British Underground Grooves" — Ramsey
& Fen's label, showcasing their own
productions with help from MJ Cole, achieved
a crossover hit with 'Love Bug' and released
loads of smooth, bouncy UKG!

THE ESSENTIALS
RAMSEY & FEN 'STYLE'
MR. JONES 'MAD CHANGES'

CATCH

1994 - 1999

One of the early UK Garage labels, bringing the Garage House sound from the States and giving it a UK twist, originally set up and run by Brian Tharme and Gavin 'DJ Face' Mills (aka Banana Republic).

THE ESSENTIALS
BANANA REPUBLIC 'CATCH THE FEELING'
THE DALKEITH CREW 'THE RIDE'

CHOCOLATE BOY

1998 - 2002

With a UK number one in 1999 from Shanks &
Bigfoot (aka Doolally), they were certainly
on a commercial tip but also had some
interesting underground Speed Garage and
darker Breakbeat Garage releases.

THE ESSENTIALS
SHANKS & BIGFOOT 'SWEET LIKE CHOCOLATE'
DJ POOCH 'BURNING UP'

CITY DUB TRAXX

1996 - 2001

One of the many side hustle sister labels from the Nice'n'Ripe group. This imprint featured classic, sought-after UK Garage tracks produced by Mike Millrain and Jeremy Sylvester under some of their many aliases.

THE ESSENTIALS
URBAN MYTHS 'MAKIN' ME FEEL'
GROOVE COMMITTEE 'HEART + SOUL'

CONFETTI RECORDS

1995 - 2001

Hands down, one of the most loved UKG labels to exist! A stomping ground for Junglists turned Garage heads like Anthill Mob (aka Studio II) and Chris Mack (Potential Bad Boy), as well as Ray Hurley and Lady Penelope.

THE ESSENTIALS
ANTHILL MOB 'FLAVA'
CHRIS MACK 'PLENTY MORE'

DEA PROJECT

1997 - 2000

Born out of Booby Trap Records and their move toward the UKG scene, the label was run by D.E.A Project (formerly known as Under Rhythm). The catalogue features stylish, jazzy 2-Step flavors throughout.

THE ESSENTIALS
D.E.A PROJECT 'SO HIGH'
D.E.A PROJECT 'LOVE ME'

DJ'S FOR LIFE

1997 - 2002

UK Garage label from Timmi Magic, Mikee B, and DJ Spoony (aka Dreem Teem), featuring heavily rotated tracks and artists such as DJ Double G, Jameson and Zed Bias—pirate radio classics galore!

THE ESSENTIALS
DJ DOUBLE G 'GET LOOSE'
KC & ZED BIAS 'LET ME KNOW (SHAKE YA THING REMIX)'

E1 RECORDINGS

1998 - 2000

Another label with only a few releases under its belt, but all absolutely hit the mark with the DJs! The label featured productions and remixes from 2's Company, Daryl B, MJ Cole and Y-Tribe.

THE ESSENTIALS
2'S COMPANY 'DESIRE'
CARROLL THOMPSON 'TOO LATE'

EC2A

2020 - PRESENT

A very prominent modern UKG label that started off with dubplate releases and made waves with artists such as Bailey Ibbs, Daffy, DJ Swagger, Main Phase and Silver Bumpa. A promising label still in its infancy!

THE ESSENTIALS
SKEPTIC 'JOIN HANDS (DARK DUB)'
VARIOUS 'CURTAIN ROAD VOL 1'

FIFTY FIRST

1995 - 2001

Quite prolific over a five-year stint,
featuring work from Antonio, DJ Deller,
Stanton Warriors, Ty Holden, and many more.
The label was not pigeonholed to one style,
covering all bases at the time!

THE ESSENTIALS
TUFF JAM 'SET IT OFF (UNDA-VYBES VOCAL MIX)'
ANTONIO 'CLOSER'

FLATTRAX

2020 - PRESENT

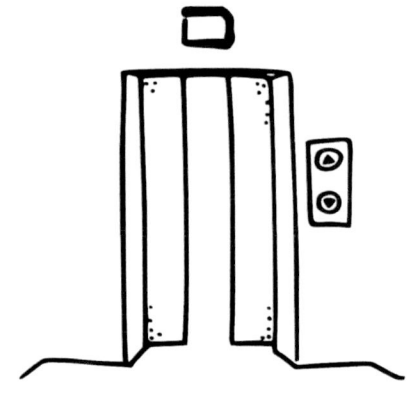

A record label set up by Highrise (aka Hardcore/Jungle producer Dwarde), releasing his own productions with guest artists on the flipsides, such as Ollie Rant, Sterling Styles, Perception, Peaky Beats and more!

THE ESSENTIALS
HIGHRISE 'TAKE ME UP'
OLLIE RANT 'IT'S YOU'

GD4YA

2018 - PRESENT

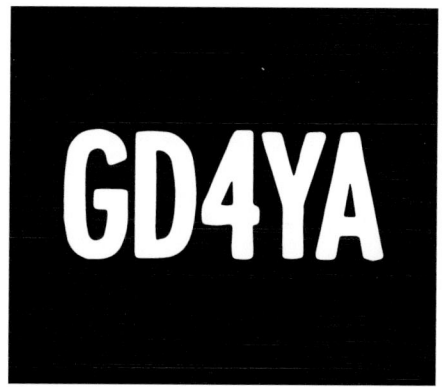

A Croydon-based label pushing UK Garage into the future, promoting new music and reissues from El-B (including his Ghost and SW2 aliases), while also serving as a platform for other rising talents, such as Yaw Evans.

THE ESSENTIALS
BENNY ILL 'SUGAR / TRIPLE S'
EL-B 'BRIXTON 2 CROYDON'

GHOST

2000 - PRESENT

An imprint started by El-B in 2000, pushing his own music, which at the time was quite dark. It went on to evolve and build the foundation for the Dubstep sound that followed in the early 2000s.

THE ESSENTIALS
GHOST 'THE CLUB'
GHOST 'DANCE HALL EP'

GROOVE CHRONICLES

1997 - 2009 / 2023

A label started by Noodles of Groove Chronicles, releasing exclusively G.C. tracks. In later years, it began reissuing garage classics by him, as well as by KMA, Steve Gurley and Zed Bias.

THE ESSENTIALS
GROOVE CHRONICLES 'STONE COLD / HOLD ON'
GROOVE CHRONICLES 'HOLIDAY DA VYBE'

HARRY LIME

2000 - 2003

Founded by Russell Fehlau, the label made an impact at the turn of the millennium within the Breakbeat / 4x4 bassline scene, mainly pushing music by Harry Lime (aka Sirus / Osmosis), Livewire and Notorious.

THE ESSENTIALS
VARIOUS 'HARRY LIME......THE ALBUM VOLUME 1'
OSMOSIS 'DRUMMAGE'

HOTPOINT

1997 - 2001

A side hustle to his Social Circles label from the legendary Jason Kaye (R.I.P), mainly released on blank labels, including releases from himself, as well as Box Clever (MJ Cole), Steve Gurley and Sticky.

THE ESSENTIALS
JASON KAYE & STEVE GURLEY 'SET IT OUT'
JASON KAYE 'SOUNDBWOY'

I! RECORDS

1997 - 2008

A legendary New York-based house label, it responsible for releasing some of the best sounds from the UK scene, featuring artists like Tuff Jam, Industry Standard, and many releases from Todd 'The God' Edwards!

THE ESSENTIALS
TUFF JAM 'KEY DUB'
VARIOUS 'EWR'

KRONIK

1998 - 2001

Originally established by Scott Garcia, this label released some of the most played UK Garage hits known to man, featuring tracks from Garcia (as Corrupted Cru), DJ Luck & MC Neat, Shy Cookie, and Troublesome.

THE ESSENTIALS
TROUBLESOME 'TROUBLESOME (DJ LUCK & SHY COOKIE RMX)'
TEMPLETON PECK 'DOWN (TEEBONE REMIX)'

LARGE JOINTS

1998 - 2001

The brainchild of Mike Milrain, this label
released a bunch of classic sample-heavy,
bootlegged R'n'B tracks in a 2-step UKG
style under his Large Joints moniker — traded
online and in record shops for top dollar!

THE ESSENTIALS
LARGE JOINTS 'DOWN ON YOU'
LARGE JOINTS & THE GREAT GATSBY 'INNER CITY BLUES'

LIFESTYLE

1998 - 2005

A short-lived effort from Jamie Williams
(Jameson/DJ Infinity) before interest came
from the majors, it put out some amazing
music that is hard to get your hands on, as
well as a couple of club anthems!

THE ESSENTIALS
JAMESON 'ALWAYS BE AROUND'
JAMESON 'URBAN HERO'

LONG LOST BROTHER

2000 - 2002

Not very well documented, but essentially artist management for S.I.A., which put out various remixes from Exemen (Wookie) and Groove Chronicles, as well as music from Kele Le Roc, Leftfoot, and Oris Jay.

THE ESSENTIALS
S.I.A 'LITTLE MAN (EXEMEN WORKS)'
S.I.A 'TAKEN FOR GRANTED (GROOVE CHRONICLES RMX)'

MONIE MUZIK

1997 - 1999

A sub-label the mighty RENK Records, which solely focused on Sky Joose's UK Garage productions, including the cult classic "I'm Getting High" - which was actually called 'Endorphins' under the SkyKap colaboration!

THE ESSENTIALS
SKYKAP 'ENDORPHINS'
SKY JOOSE 'THE JOOSE EP'

NEW DEAL

2000 - 2003

Providing artillery for the Breakbeat Garage scene in the early 2000s, Shut Up & Dance's sub-label released club classics, all produced by the legendary production duo Carlton Hyman and Philip Johnson.

THE ESSENTIALS
1 UP FRONT 'HOLD TIGHT'
YOUNGSTAR 'TRUE VIP!'

NICE'N'RIPE

1993 - 2001

One of the most well-known and loved UKG labels, instrumental in the formative years of the scene, it was founded by Grant Nelson and helped birth over 30 smaller labels, making it the most collected label in the scene.

THE ESSENTIALS
24HOUR EXPERIENCE 'PART TWO: MORE DUB ESSENTIALS'
THE RHYTHM CONSTRUCTION CO. 'TEST PRESS'

NORTH WEST 10

1996 - 2002

Founded by Ali Jawando of Y-Tribe, this House and UK Garage imprint released cuts exclusively by the Y-Tribe duo, who had a crossover hit with their Restless Natives project. There's some serious wax on this label!

THE ESSENTIALS
RESTLESS NATIVES 'THE KALAKUTA E.P'
Y-TRIBE FT. ELIZABETH TROY 'ENOUGH IS ENOUGH'

POINT BLANK

2000 -2005

Known for a massive hit with The Wideboys, the label also featured Ray Hurley and Groove Chronicles. It recently reopened to promote newer talents, as well as old school heads Si Firmin and Crazy Bank.

THE ESSENTIALS
WIDEBOYS 'WESTSIDE'
GROOVE CHRONICLES 'RETRO EP'

QUENCH

1997 - 2002

Sister label to Thirst & Moist, it was founded by Danny Donnelly (Suburban Base) and run by DJ Lewi. The label put out a range of heavy hitters from the likes of Anthill Mob, DJ Lewi and Underground Solution.

THE ESSENTIALS
ANTHILL MOB 'DON'T LEAVE ME'
ORDINARY PEOPLE 'BUBBLIN' SOUND'

RELENTLESS

1999 - 2004

Heavily pushing UKG into the mainstream
at the end of the '90s, it was key to the
success and popularity of acts such as Artful
Dodger, Daniel Bedingfield, Mark Ryder,
So Solid Crew and Wiley - to name but a few.

THE ESSENTIALS
MARK 'RUFF' RYDER 'JOY'
PHAZE ONE 'NICOLE'S GROOVE'

S2S RECORDINGS

2000 - 2001

That's right; Soul II Soul! Jazzie B's label focused on jumpstarting Wookie's career as a garage act, helping to get his album to mass appeal and giving crossover success to what is now a household name!

THE ESSENTIALS
WOOKIE FT. LAIN 'BATTLE'
WOOKIE 'WHAT'S GOING ON?'

SHUFFLE'N'SWING

2019 - PRESENT

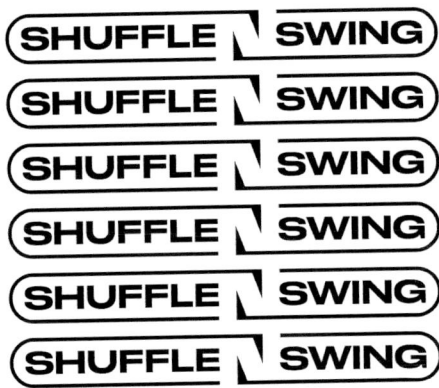

A group of UK Garage fanatics has built a label around a growing online community, releasing both - rare old garage reissues and promoting brand-new talents like Harry Luda, Highrise and Pure Sleek!

THE ESSENTIALS
GUSH COLLECTIVE 'SHUFFLE'N'SWING 001'
CUTMASTER ACE 'LONDON VIBES / ESCAPE'

SMOKIN BEATS

1996 - 2003

Founded by Paul Landon and Neil Rumney (aka Zoom & DBX), who go by many names, including Smokin Beats, the label released more house-influenced UK Garage from themselves as well as other emerging artists in the mid to late '90s.

THE ESSENTIALS
SMOKIN BEATS 'DREAMS'
SMOKIN BEATS 'JAZZ HOUSE (DOPE MIX)'

TIMEHRI

2021 - 2023

A London-based imprint from T. Dunn, featuring a small but solid catalog of new school mainstays such as Highrise, DJ Perception, Thunderkats and Yosh. Hopefully, there will be more to come!

THE ESSENTIALS
DJ PERCEPTION 'FUTURE HORIZONS EP'
THE THUNDERKATS 'WORMHOLE DOJO EP'

UNIT FIVE

1998 - 2002

Red Rose Recordings' sister label, pushing a more underground sound with original music and remixes from Alpha Omega (aka Oracles), Dub Syndicate, Ed Case, JJ Louis, MJ Cole and The Wideboys.

THE ESSENTIALS
ALPHA OMEGA 'RHYTHM TAKES CONTROL'
JJ LOUIS & JADE LION - RUFF TUFF 'N' READY

URBAN BEAT

1995 - 1997

Highly underground, classy, and dubby
UK Garage jams from the likes of Baffled,
Dangerous Minds, KMA Productions and SFX
which fetch good money on the second-hand
market - and all in need of a repress!

THE ESSENTIALS
KMA PRODUCTIONS 'PHANTASY TRIP / CAPE FEAR'
BAFFLED 'GOING ON'

SOUTHSIDECIRCULARS.COM